Dark Side of You

I0201087

A. Salter

sAw Publishing

*Dedicated to
Larry, Olive and Carrington, who
taught me that reality can be an
opinion.*

I

I was haunted by you.

A thousand creatures.

Some I know not.

All is said and done.

Nothing can reverse time.

None can change the past.

What has already been completed.

No one can change people.

Except you.

For you can do all.

And none can stop you.

You

Your life was wonderful.

Full of love,
joy,
gladness,
contentment.

Your children were beautiful.
Perfect reflections of you.

Your wife was full of joy and love for you and her
family.

But.

There is always an exception.

Sickness and death soon plagued your home.

Wiped out many.

You never would have thought
that you would soon be
the administrator of death,
the dealer of disease.

But,

Just now, all you wanted was to be saved.
You and your family.

Your wants,

your needs,
were all cast aside.
Ignored.

Never to be seen again.
Never to be considered.
None are merciful.

Not ever.

These were the thoughts that held you captive.

Your children's existence,
life force,
love,
fade into nothing.

But

Death is a mercy you could never afford.

You watched as the plagues left your home an empty
shell of its former glory.

Nothing good left behind.

Love is just a fading undertaking, destined to fail.
Happiness a brief oasis for the distraught.

Family didn't last.

Not for you.
Never for you.

You watch as your wife slips into madness.

Clawing.
Screaming.
Wasting her life away.

Haunted by memory.

Forever haunted.

Her mumbles of nonsense,
Her inaudible cries.
Her pain.

She was only a hollow reminder
of the woman she used to be.

The mother,
for one cannot be a mother without her children.

Your distress only amplified by the knives.

The unhealthy obsession.

The blood escaping her veins from numerous slices
and scratches.

Fascinated,
both of you were,

but for different reasons.

Always different reasons.

The months turned to years as time flew out of your
grasp.

You wanted it to be over.

Over forever.

Eternal relief.
Eternal family.
Eternal love.

But do not be fooled.
Nothing goes as planned.
Not for you.

Never again.

Entering your home for the last time,
you were not surprised
to find your wife hanging from the roof.

Her eyes void of the madness.
Void of the love.

She was happier now.
With her children.
But away from you.

Compromise comes with payment.
She paid with you.

Not for much longer.
You will follow her example.
You crave the relief as she had.

The loneliness was familiar to you.
You had been alone for years.

Madness stole her from you.
Madness stole your life.
Your love.
Your will.

You rejoice when you felt the noose tighten,
choking out the life you no longer wanted.

You wanted death.
You needed it.
You knew of nothing else.

There was nothing left for you here.

Nothing left.

You have no more hope.

None here.

Love floods you one final time as you fade into blackness,
your body swinging next to her.

Searching.
The first thing you do
after you cross the threshold.

For family.
For yourself.

Fear is what most would feel.
But not by you.

Never you.

Your eyes wander the dull landscape,
looking for those stolen from you.

Willingly or not.
You didn't care.
You only want them back.

But your luck had run out.

Did you ever have any luck to start with?

Or the worst luck of all?

Your hope leaving you more and more every moment
you are alone.

"Your destiny has found you," an echoing voice calls
to you.

You look around.

The speaker is not in sight.

You are alone.

"Look at your new body," it says again,
quieter this time.
Much quieter.
As if it was in your head
and your head alone.

You look at your hands and are unsurprised.
The sickly flesh spread across your bones.
Concealing the bloodless veins webbed throughout
your body.

"Commit yourself to your new purpose," the voice
says.
The voice is your own.

But it is different.
Harder.
Rougher.
Less feeling.

Words forming sentences you both know and don't.
Both familiar and foreign.

"Reaper."

You are powerful.
You are no longer suppressed.
No longer in pain.

You need no others.

You forsake your fruitless search.
You have found something better.

You cross the threshold
back into life.

You carry death.
Suffering.
Pain.
Disease.

You unleash plagues among villages.

Once happy homes.
They end like your life did.

But you remember nothing now.
Only the pain.

You collect the dead as they pour into your domain.
Unchecked.

All you touch is history.

But you are still alone.

Forever alone.

Order.
This is something you despise.

The peace.
The joy.
The absence of chaos.

It drives you mad.

You can't tolerate it,
you destroy it.

Your victims can do nothing to stop you
as you uproot their lives.
Steal them away.

They are yours now.
They've always been yours.

With tempting words that none can resist.

Words of death.
Hatred.
Pain.

Eternal pain.

They would be better without this life.

They believe you.

Fools.

They string themselves up,

one by one.
Burdened with only hope.

No regrets.

But they will not be disappointed,
for they will soon drown in despair.

They will feel that regret for eternity.

When they cross the threshold,
they are refugees,
simply looking for a better life.

They came to the wrong place.
They are stuck.
There is no way back.

None can cross the threshold twice.

None but you.
You have free reign.
No order here.
Only chaos.
Anarchy.
Punishment.

Your cages hold the disobedient.
Other than them,
none know your true intentions

None know the peril they're in.

None know their future.
Their lives are at stake.

But are they alive?

No.

Then their sanity is at stake.
Their joy.
Their very existence.

Everything and anything they cherish will be ripped apart.

Burned.
Drowned.
Utterly destroyed.

But they don't know that.
Not yet.

They feel safe.
They feel at home.

But they are not at home.
They never will be.
Not again.

They are not safe.
They will find out soon enough.

But not soon enough for you.

You hasten their pain.

They think you are helping them,
but you are destroying them.

When the defiant ones arrive,
oh, and arrive they will,
you will have punishment ready.

Cages.
So many assumptions, implications.

None are true.

Can one be caged willingly?

A chorus of silence reaches your ears.

"But why not?" You ask yourself
Why not?

For cages can keep one safe.
Keep things out.
Keep things in.

A cage can become one's home.
One's paradise.
One's escape.

Not always an imprisonment,
not always torture.

"It will be fun," you whisper seductively in their ears.
"Just follow me,
to be set free."

They follow you unknowingly.
They trust you,
foolishly.
For persuasion is one of your many gifts,
a talent even.

But is it persuasion?

You herd them across your threshold.
Into your world of eternal pain, hate, suffering.

There is no death.
All is eternal.

The horizon great.
A sphere.
An endless trek.

Without change,
without end.

Your reign is absolute.
Your throne holds no other.
The crown is for you alone.

They have learned the punishment for betrayal.

Severe, they are.
Severe, they've always been.

But greater now,
for greater power calls for greater fear.

Isolation is what you hand them.

"Not so bad." They think at first.
"Not so bad."

What a shallow word.

Bad

For it does nothing to encompass eternal loneliness.

Nothing can.
Nothing ever will.
You made sure of that.

First comes the darkness.

Black as tar.
Darker than night.
Emptier than void.

But not as black as your heart.

Nothing is that dark.
Nothing is that empty.

Victims scream at first,
but soon realize that they are soundless.

Second comes the silence.
Sound cut off.

The only thing that can be heard is your laughter.

Your unquenchable thirst for pain,

for suffering.

Third comes the wait.

In silence and darkness.

Praying for death.
Death that will not come.
Never come.

You are a merciless captor,
one that knows nothing of relief, feelings, emotion.

You only know pain and torture.

They beg for death,
but you cannot grant it.

One cannot die twice.

They have asked for death before.
As have all under your reign.

You had been merciful once,
when you were one of them.
When you granted their last request.

They used to hate and despair,
Now they live and prosper.

Completely unaware of your true intent.
Your deception.

Your treachery.

Unknowingly walking into your trap.

More every day.
More and more.

A smile distorts your features,
disguising your ruthless cruelty.

You snap your fingers and more appear.

You laugh.

The unsuspecting victims laugh with you,
unknowing that it is at the expense of their future.

They cry with joy when they see you return.

But you know all.

Their cries will soon be muted.

Their fears unmasked
in the unseeing oblivion.

Their screams unheard in the deafening silence.

They have no understanding of the pain, suffering,
hate that you have endured.
That you will make them endure.

"Come this way," you say, looking at your subjects.

They follow you willingly.
Toward a fate worse than death.
All fate is worse than death,
for death is the utmost form of mercy.

"Come this way," you say again,
suppressing your humorless mirth.

"It will be fun."

The first one enters your cage gladly.
A gladness that will soon be vanquished.

The others less so,
for they feel a different type of anticipation.

But you are not to be defied,
they know what happens to the hopeful.

Their cries of joy are screams of fear as the darkness
descends upon them.

They cannot hear their cries
for silence assaults their unhearing ears.

Your laughter is their only companion.

The hopeless wait for eternity to pass will commence
as they fade forever into oblivion.

The feverish gaze of passing foes
uncertain of your intent.
Screaming as they fall, unheard by all
except by their dying lover's ears.

Merciless Thief you were once named
by the Grieving Widow's tongue,
her incriminating words going to waste upon deaf
ears.

They're more meaningless than the feelings you once
had felt,
rotting away at blackened hearts.

Walking from the pain, suffering and disease
you had brought in your wake.
You suppress a laugh at the Grieving Widow for she
means nothing.

Death brings you joy now.
Only death.

Stopping you is beyond ability
for seeing is death, and pain, and disease.

There is no stopping sight,
therefore, no stopping you.

The feeling less expression that coats your face,
shielding from overcoming emotion.

This shall save you, as it has before,

keeping you alone.

As you like it.

No longer a Merciless Thief,
For the Grieving Widow has been silenced.

Her eyes empty, sunken orbs.
Vacant of feeling.
They show no victory nor loss.

Her tongue a shriveled corpse.
Vile tasting and speaks of nothing.

Her skin a dull shell of the fruitful life it had once
held.
Her heart no less shattered than it used to be.

Death's horrid influence raged upon all except the
soul,
which shines with an unknown radiance beyond the
grave.

She is much happier now,
for she is no longer at your mercy.

You cannot pass the threshold of death a second
time.
You would be imprisoned.

Just as so many before you,
just as the Grieving Widow who grieves no longer.

Your macabre appearance can only strike fear in the
hearts of the living.
Death is a fate that none can outrun.

Its ominous figure haunting at every opportunity.

Long ago, when you used to care,
when you used to appear the same as most.

Your reflection showed the average husband.
The average Father.
The average son.

Mirrors often lie,
for the reflection is how one views oneself.

But, now, after all has passed, you are different.
Some see you as a formless, faceless mask.
Others see you as a gateway to the ones they have
lost.
But most see you as the elusive thief who steals what
isn't yours to take.

As did the Grieving Widow,
a victim of the greatest crime one could comprehend.

Her hurting soul, her violated emotions, her broken
heart
all pale in comparison to her deepest sense of loss.

But loss passes quickly when you are there to help it
on its way.

Just as the Grieving Widow feels no more loss,
you feel no more guilt,
no more pain, suffering, disease.

You only cause it now.
You can only hurt the ones in life.
The ones in that brief horizon of temporary joy.

The stage that disguises all forms of torture.
Having them look appealing, beautiful even.

Captivating, like a moth to the flame,
only to have their life burned out when they get too
close.

You are the flame
the Grieving Widow, the moth, for she cannot resist
your temptation.

The wills of men are weak
the wills of the grieving are even weaker still.

They miss, overcome by loss and can think of nothing
else.

Some will come to you willingly,
others will have to be taken by force.

You favor the willing ones.

You watch their slow decline with a sickening glee in
your eye.
A morbid smile splitting your face.

You delight in their pain.
Partake in their demise.

You watch as they choose between the knife or the
noose.
They are unaware you had made that decision for
them long ago.
Before you put thoughts of death in their rapidly
diminishing minds.

You see them slit and stab, tie and hang.
Then join you on your side of the threshold.

They are eternally at peace,
but the loss has been passed to their lovers,
their Grieving Widows when they are found.

Hanging from the roof.
Sprawled upon the floor,
their blood creating a permanent stain on all it
touches.

You laugh gleefully at their screams for Death is
contagious.

They are next.

You are an unstoppable sickness,
a plague worth reckoning.
There is no antidote nor immunity.

You will receive all,
just as you obtained the Grieving Widow.
But she was strong of will, unlike the willing ones.
She refused to let you gain the upper hand.

"Merciless Thief." She spat at your unfeeling face.
"Even you cannot escape death forever."

With one touch of your hand, she fell to the ground.
Her eyes staring back at you with a look only the dead
can achieve.

You are used to that look,
and you feel joyous when you witness it.

"Another job well done." It seems to say to you.

The Grieving Widow has no power now,
for she is one of your subjects.
One of the dead.

Merciless Thief

It echoes in your cold heart.
The heart that used to be alive and warm.

Before loss sunk its claws into your soul.
Before your wife became one of the willing ones.

Before you became one of the willing ones.

Merciless Thief

The words beckon to you in a way you have never felt.

Was it guilt?
Regret?

No. You feel nothing.

Merciless Thief

The Grieving Widow calls to you as her memory takes hold of your mind.

How could the administrator of death become haunted by death itself?

Merciless Thief

You look at your hand.
Its sickly, pale flesh nauseates you.

None could live like this.
One could only die like this.

Merciless Thief

Your freezing heart,
your devious mind.
Your soul.

They mean nothing to this world.
Only to bring death, pain, suffering, disease.

Merciless Thief

Your mind recalls every terrible, unimaginable
feeling of loss that you had thrust into a mind.
A mind that had been still full of life,
but was now practicality drowning in death and
despair.

Merciless Thief

There was too much.
Too much chaos.
Too much pain.
Too much suffering.
Too much loss.

Merciless Thief

The Grieving Widow taunted relentlessly from the
other side.

Merciless Thief

You thrust your hand onto your chest.
The chest that was vacant of any and all feeling.

No love.
No hope.

No joy.
Only death.

Merciless Thief

Giving yourself a dose of your own craft.
You feel for the first time since life.

Merciless Thief

The chuckle of the Grieving Widow was all that could
be heard by your newly opened ears.

Merciless Thief

You realize.
You feel.
You see what you have done,
all the loss you have caused.
All the pain, suffering, disease.

Even the death.
For death is inevitable,
even to those who administer it.

Left behind was a better world.
No more loss, pain, suffering, disease.

For there was no more death.
For there was no more you.

But with no more death, this brief horizon of
temporary joy became
a permanent prison of all-encompassing chaos.

You stand by, laughing aloud as crime runs wild.
As life begins to hold no meaning for it will never
end.

Your mirth is only fueled by the willing ones who live
in eternal pain.
They know they will only begin to live when they are
one of the dead.

You embrace the pain that has taken them captive.
You know that their deepest desires,
their most heartfelt wishes,
will one day come true.

For death cannot keep its master prisoner.

Years crawl by.
They may be able to stop you,
but none can stop time.

Time is your companion,

Time helps the strong of will on their way
to make up their minds.

Nothing can reverse the feeble mortality of all living
beings.

Nothing but you.

But you aren't living.
You haven't lived for an age.
Not anymore.

The longer you wait,
the stronger you become.

Nothing can avert you from your cause.

Nothing can distract you from your sinful desires.

Your addictions.
Your lustful attitude.
Your unhealthy obsession.

Your mind is set.

Nothing can change your destiny.

Not even you.

You begin to feel a tug.

You've felt this before and you embrace it joyously.

It pulls you back across the threshold.
The doorway you have been unable to cross again.

Laughing at the fear they feel.
For it radiates off them in waves.

They all know you are back.
Even if none can see you.

You take the first one you see.

It revolts you to think you were once mortal.

Such fragile beings
with wills that are all the more delicate.

One touch from you and they will shatter.

Everything and anything will die.
Living or not.
You watch as forests fade.
Towns vacate.
Bodies rot.

The victims who run are no safer
for you are everywhere.

You know all.
See all.
But feel nothing.

Nothing can penetrate your cold facade.

Your excitement elevates when you feel your realm
fill.

You have been dormant for far too long.

Your hunger has not been quieted.

You want more.

Always more.

Unabating.
Never ceasing.
Unable to stop.
That's all right with you.
You're not the one paying dearly for your joy.

Paying with their lives.
Nothing is free.
Not for them.

Not when you are charging.

Not when the costs are so high.

You feel the best you've ever felt.

You are in your element.
You will never leave it again.

There is nothing one can do.
None can persuade you.

You are home.

And all will soon despair.

For you will win.
You will always win.

A Victim

You were invited.
You came.
Loyal.

As you've always done.
Always been there for them.

Always.

Now, you hope they will be there for you.

But you were wrong.
Always wrong.

About everything.

The love they portrayed.
The care they conveyed.

All fake.
Always fake.
Nothing was real.
Not ever.

As you wait you feel cold.
Something frozen caresses your heart.

It dripped and pooled down at your feet.

Movement was impossible
as you slowly drown.

Alone.
Without aid.
Always alone.

Loyal you no longer were.
Loyal you will never be again.

Kindness a feeling,
now foreign.
Compassion deserted you.
Love forsake you.

Just as your family did.
Your friends.
All you hold dear.

Gone.

For you mean nothing to them.

"Did you ever?"
You wonder quietly,
"Did your death mean nothing?"
"Could they continue?"

For you surely would have followed in their footsteps.

Met death with open arms,
letting him consume you.

Your will would be weak

if it wasn't for them.

They are now gone.
Gone forever.

Your will went with them.

As would you.
You would do anything.

But there is nothing you can do.

Except for revenge.

You planned for months.
Years.
Decades.
You have time to wait.
Time to spare.
Here, time matters not.

Time no longer exists.

But you cannot pass through the threshold between
the living and the dead.
Not again.

You only know one who can.

The one who stole you from life.
Planted thoughts in your head.

You came to Death.

"No," you tell yourself.
"I was in control."
"I was always in control."
Always.

But you know it is a lie.

No control is yours.
Nothing is yours.

Except your revenge.

You see Death leaving his cages.

Those horrible houses of punishment.

None truly know what takes place there.

One can only guess.
That you've done.
All have guessed.
But none are right.

You see Death coming your way.
The reaper.
The mask.
The Thief.

Merciless Thief.

Death steals all.

You inform Death of your need.

Death laughs gleefully,
but there is something hidden within his facade.

Something sinister.

You choose not to know.
Death chooses not to share.

Death vanishes in a cloud of darkness.

Pain.
Suffering.
Disease.

But it can't harm you here.
Nothing can.
Nothing ever will.

Death will find them,
your betrayers.

They will share your life.
Your pain.
Your suffering.
Your fate.

You will share theirs.

You will be bound to your worst enemy.

After their horrific death at the hands of Death
himself.

Upon your orders,
and your orders alone.

You watch as death spoils the betrayers' minds.
Bringing them to their knees.

But not too quickly.

You want them to suffer.
They will suffer eternally through your shared fates.

Never alone again.

Never.

They suffer for years.

Long after Death has left their minds.

But not permanently.
He will be back.

Death is never absent.

Not in the strongest of will,
nor in the most willing of men.

He is unstoppable.

He squashes all good out of them.
They turn on one another.

Killing with words.
Killing with fists.
Murderers.

They display all men are known for.

They are weak.

You laugh at the weakness you no longer feel.

Forgetting that you were once like them.
That you still are.

You will no longer suffer through their flaws.

Their mortality.
Their fallibility.
Their frailty.

The pure despair that floods their bodies as Death
returns to their mind.

They knew he would be back.

You anticipate their fall more than anything.

All else vacates your mind.

Nothing else matters.

You forget the evil glint in Death's eye.
His double-crossing plots.
You are unaware of your own demise.
Your pending expiration.

You shut it out,
for surely none can harm you here.

None that you would expect.

Not Death.
For he has already hurt you once.

You bask in their pain as their life lights are
extinguished.

You scream with delight as they pass through the threshold as you had once done.

As you will never do again.

They kneel before you,
begging for mercy.

But what they had done was inexcusable.
Forgiveness is no longer in your vocabulary.

Death was not pleased,
seeing the pain you caused.

That crime was for him to commit.
Him alone.

He did not approve of your methods for they were
alike to his own.

With a grin painted across his face
and a snap of his fingers,
you were in a cage.

The only punishment,
but so many combined.

There was no return.
No return for you.

Your betrayers followed you to your fate,
for your two fates were now one.

There was no escape.
Only exile.

You wonder how you missed it.

The look of pure malice that Death wore as a crown.
The sadistic need to see others in pain.
To see lives ripped apart.

Mothers torn from their children.

Husbands leaving their wives in hopes of a better life
across the threshold.

There is no life beyond the threshold.

Only death.
Only you.

But you were happy.
Even in this place of only sorrow.

For revenge was now yours.

You listened to the screams of your betrayer as
darkness took you captive.

The only sound was Death's laughter.
Or was it your laughter?

Your two voices mixed and clashed,
Sounding like a symphony with the voice of demons.

Your betrayer only screamed louder.
And Death only laughed harder.

Next came the silence.

This, nothing could have prepared you for.

No screams were heard.
No laughter rang.

Only the shouts of silence.
Only the feeling of despair lingered.

None could rid you of that feeling.
For none else remained.

None could tell how quickly time passed for eternity
has no measurement.

Time ceased to exist.
Feeling fled your diminishing body.

Did you still have a body?
You cared not.

The wait was unbearable.

Your skin was ash,
blowing in the wind,
its fire long been extinguished.

Nothing could offer you relief.
For the torment you underwent was unbearable.

You could no longer hear your betrayer's screams.
No longer witness their suffering.

The only suffering you were aware of was your own.

But you were content.
For your betrayer followed in your footsteps.

Death didn't blink an eye when you and your betrayer faded past the final threshold,
where you would be tortured until the end of eternity.

You felt nothing as you fell.
Deeper and deeper.
Through the threshold none knew was there.

Except Death himself.
For nothing is unknown in his own domain.
Nothing is kept secret.
Not from him.

His centuries spent were not wasted.

Death is wiser than all things.
Nothing has ever caught him unaware.
Unsuspecting.

Except for one thing.

The Grieving Widow has resided where you now fall.
The third threshold.
The unknown punishment.
Impossibly worse than the cages.

Everything can get worse.

Merciless Thief

She still haunts him.
She still pays dearly for it.
She always will.

As you fall, you think of nothing but escape.
But it is impossible.

Where time wouldn't be the end of you.
Time's rays don't reach that far into the abyss.

Nothing can touch you there.
Only him.
For you are in his favorite domain.
The one he only visits for you.
And her.

You are still curious.
Who could bring Death over the edge?
Who could bring a flood of guilt to one so far gone?
Who could bring one so powerful toward so much
despair?

You landed suddenly,
next to your betrayer.

They move no more,
as their essence retreats back to the second threshold.

None can cross twice.
Not without Death's permission.

He didn't want your enemy.
He only wants you.

Death will always get what he wants.

He finds you and whispers.

"You are alone. None can find you where you have
fallen."

Hopelessness and despair assault you.
You gasp for breath when the pain hits.
Harder and harder.
More painful by the minute.

For nothing hurts you more than being alone.
Than having no one to comfort you.

You used to have your revenge to rely on.
But now,
you have nothing.

Only death.
Pain.
Suffering.

But you are not completely alone.
For the Grieving Widow is with you.
She endures the same as you.

Only worse.
Forever worse.

The anxiety that envelops you is contagious.
The Grieving Widow starts feeling it too.

But not for herself.
She is not as selfish as you.
She fears for you.
For she knows what to expect.
She has been subjected to it for lifetimes.

You cannot cope with the brutal reality.
She has seen people like you.

People who care for none but themselves.
They relish only in the pain of others.
The pain that they cause.

You remind her of him.
Of Death.

He stole from her,
a crime that cannot be forgiven.
Will never be forgiven.

She cares not for the torture Death subjects her to.
Only for the ones stolen from her.
She cares for you too,
even if she despises your kind.

She cannot change herself.
None can change people.
Not even the most willing ones.
They are to remain how they were created.
Forever.

Death approaches you, unaware of the Grieving
Widow's interference.
The strength she still possesses goes unnoticed.

Death whispers meaningless words in your
vulnerable ears.
They were unaware of the pain that envelops them
for you are broken.
You are weak.

But the Grieving Widow has much greater strength.
Will.
Purpose.
Reason.

She will never break.
Not until she has broken Death himself.

Death turns to her, long after you had faded into
darkness,
never to return.

He looks at her eyes,
still so filled with life.

He sees nothing but determination.
Nothing but joy.

Nothing he had ever seen.
Not so deep in his clutches.

There is not a trace of fear in her eyes.

Her posture speaks of nothing but a firm resolve.

She will vanquish Death again.
And this time, he will never return.

Me

I didn't know what to make of you,
so powerful was your demise.

You were there one moment.
Then you were gone.

You were inches away from having me in your
clutches.
Nothing could have brought me back.

I was gone.
Already faded.

Hope was no longer a possibility,
for it would have been a lie.

My confusion only intensified the better I got.

But is it good you are gone,
never to return?

You kept us in line.
Although your methods were occasionally
questionable
and your motives immoral,
you did us a service.

You gave life value.
Even though you value nothing.

You let us live.
Even though you killed us.

You gave us a time frame.
Even though you cut it short.

Without you I have no meaning.
No purpose.
No reason to justify existence.

One always needs a reason.
A reason to live.

After you were destroyed,
everything was nothing.

Nothing was worth anything.
Nothing was enough.

We needed you.
Or someone like you.
To do the job none else would.

Soon, I felt the calling,
as you once had felt.

The calling that had aided in your destruction.
The calling that had stolen your life.
Your love.
Your family.
Your will.

You were nothing without it,

and even less with it.

Without that calling,
the earth would fall deeper in despair.
The cycle must continue.

The calling must always be answered.
By you or me,
it matters not.
It could be any of us.

I intended to follow in your footsteps,
but I would be better than you.

I would not share your fate.

I would not relish in the demise of others.

People would be grateful for me.

They would call me their merciful Thief.

Merciful Thief

www.ingramcontent.com/pod-product-compliance
Lightning Source LLC
Chambersburg PA
CBHW021144020426
42331CB00005B/885